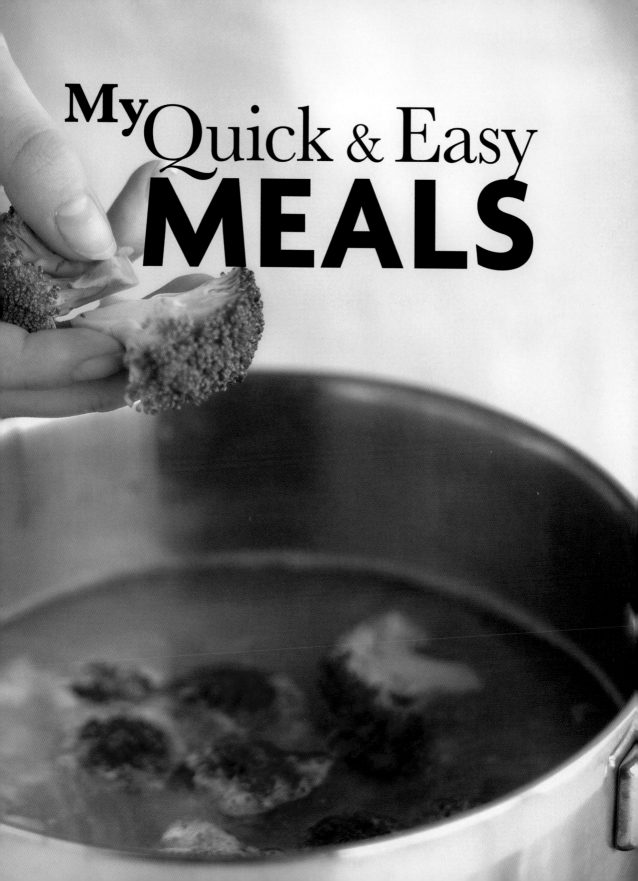

My Quick & Easy MEALS

My Quick & Easy MEALS

Written by Nicola Graimes, Katharine Ibbs and Denise Smart
Photography by Howard Shooter

COVENT
GARDEN
BOOKS

COVENT
GARDEN
BOOKS

Senior Editor Ros Walford
Production Editor Kavita Varma
Senior Designer Lisa Crowe
Editors Heather Scott, Julia March, Elizabeth Noble
Designers Dan Bunyan, Justin Greenwood,
Lynne Moulding, Thelma-Jane Robb
Production Controller Pieta Pemberton
Home Economists Katharine Ibbs, Denise Smart
Assistant Home Economists Fergal Connolly, Lisa Harrison, Sarah Tildesley
Consultant Nicola Graimes
Publishing Managers Simon Beecroft, Cynthia O'Neill Collins
Category Publisher Alex Allan/Siobhan Williamson

Published in Great Britain in 2012 by
Dorling Kindersley Limited,
80 Strand, London, WC2R 0RL
Penguin Group (UK)

Contains content from *Children's Cookbook* (2004),
Children's Healthy & Fun Cookbook (2007) and *Cookbook for Girls* (2009)

10 9 8 7 6 5 4 3 2 1
003–182285–Aug/12

A CIP catalogue record for this book is available from the British Library.

ISBN: 978-1-4053-7403-3

Reproduced by Media Development and Printing Ltd., UK
Printed and bound in China by South China Printing Co. Ltd

Contents

Strawberry Scrunch

Toasted oats and seeds add crunchiness to this layered breakfast, and provide important nutrients too. The yoghurt is a low-fat source of protein and calcium, while the strawberries and orange juice are rich in vitamin C. Honey adds sweetness, but you could use maple syrup instead.

Tasty Twists

Swap the strawberries for your favourite fruits such as bananas, nectarines, or peaches. Fruit purée also taste great!

Ingredients

- 150g (5¹/₂oz) strawberries (about 6-8)
- 4 tbsp fresh orange juice
- 50g (2oz) whole porridge oats
- 3 tbsp sunflower seeds
- 3 tbsp pumpkin seeds
- 2-3 tbsp clear runny honey
- 12 dsp thick natural bio yoghurt

pumpkin seeds

honey

strawberries

Equipment

- small sharp knife
- chopping board
- small bowl
- frying pan
- wooden spoon

chopping board

1 Cut the green stalks and leaves from the strawberries and then thickly slice the fruit. Put the strawberries in a bowl and add the orange juice. Set aside.

2 Put the oats in a frying pan and dry fry over a medium-low heat for 3 mins. Turn the oats occasionally with a wooden spoon to make sure they cook evenly.

3 Next add the sunflower and pumpkin seeds and dry fry for another 2 minutes or until light golden. Take care the pumpkin seeds may pop a little!

This would also make a great-tasting dessert!

Food Facts

Oats are a carbohydrate food. They are perfect for breakfast because the fibre in them is digested by the body slowly. This makes you feel full for longer and keeps your blood sugar levels steady. Oats are also a great source of vitamins E, B1, and B2.

oats

4 Take the pan off the heat. Stir in the honey – it will sizzle at first but keep stirring until the oats and seeds are coated. Allow to cool slightly.

5 Put a layer of the oats in the bottom of each glass. Add 2 heaped dessert spoonfuls of yoghurt and then some of the fruit. Add another layer of each.

Breakfast Tortilla

A tortilla is a thick, flat omelette and is a popular dish in Spain. This is a twist on the classic combination of eggs, onion, and potatoes and makes a filling breakfast or perfect after-school tea.

Did you know?
"Tortilla" is the Spanish word for omelette. In Italy it is called "frittata". However, in Mexico, "tortilla" means a thin (unleavened) bread usually made from corn.

Ingredients

eggs

- 4 good quality sausages (or vegetarian alternative)
- 4 medium-sized potatoes (peeled, cooked and left to cool)
- 2 tbsp sunflower oil

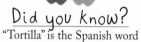
cherry tomatoes   potatoes

- 8 cherry tomatoes (halved)
- 5 eggs (lightly beaten)
- salt and pepper

Equipment

- foil
- tongs
- chopping board
- medium frying pan
- spatula or wooden spoon
- jug
- whisk or fork
- small sharp knife

frying pan

spatula

1 Preheat the grill to medium-high. Line the grill pan with foil and grill the sausages all over for 10-15 mins, or until cooked through and golden brown.

2 While the sausages are cooling slightly, cut the cooked potatoes into bite-sized chunks. Then cut the cooled sausages into 2.5cm (1in) pieces.

Tasty Twists

Vegetarian sausages, lean bacon, or cooked chicken would also taste great in this tortilla. Other vegetables such as mushrooms, peppers, or asparagus could also be added.

3 Heat the oil in a frying pan. Add the potatoes and fry them over a medium heat for 8 minutes or until golden. Add the tomatoes and cook for 2 mins.

4 Crack the eggs into a jug and then beat them together. Season the beaten eggs with salt and pepper. Add the sausages to the frying pan.

5 Add a little more oil to the frying pan if necessary. Pour the eggs into the pan and cook, without stirring, for 5 minutes until the base of the tortilla is set.

6 To cook the top of the tortilla, carefully place the pan under the grill and cook for another 3–5 minutes, or until the top is set.

7 Carefully remove the pan from the grill and leave to cool slightly before sliding the tortilla on to a serving plate. Cut into wedges and serve.

Griddle Cakes

These American-style savoury pancakes are perfect for a light but filling meal or as a tasty weekend brunch.

Helpful Hints

Keep the bacon and cooked pancakes warm in the oven while you cook the rest of the griddle cakes. They are delicious served with guacomole.

Did you know?

Corn is a member of the grass family so it isn't really a vegetable, it's a grain. The average ear of sweetcorn has 800 kernels, arranged in 16 rows.

Ingredients

wholemeal flour

- 110g (4oz) plain flour, white, or wholemeal
- 1 tsp bicarbonate of soda
- 1 tsp baking powder
- 1 free-range egg
- 100ml (3½ fl oz) milk
- 75g (3oz) sweetcorn (frozen or tinned)

- 284ml carton buttermilk
- 1 tsp sunflower oil
- 8 lean bacon rashers
- salt and pepper

bacon

sweetcorn

Equipment

whisk

- small jug
- fork or whisk
- sieve
- large mixing bowl
- wooden spoon
- tin foil
- large frying pan
- ladle
- spatula

frying pan

1 Pour the milk into a jug and then carefully crack the egg straight into the jug. Mix the milk and egg together with a fork or small whisk.

2 Sift the flour, bicarbonate of soda, baking powder and a pinch of salt into a large mixing bowl. Make a well in the centre of the bowl.

3 Pour the milk and egg mixture into the well into the centre of the flour mixture. Then carefully add the buttermilk and sweetcorn.

4 Gently beat the mixture until the ingredients are combined. Cover the mixture with a plate and leave to stand while you cook the bacon.

5 Line the grill rack with foil and preheat the grill to medium. Put the bacon under the grill and cook for 2–3 minutes on each side, or until crisp.

6 Heat the oil in the pan and then ladle in the batter to make griddle cakes about 10cm (4in) in diameter. Make sure there is space between the cakes.

7 Cook for 2–3 minutes, until golden underneath. Flip and then cook the other side. Make 12 cakes in this way, adding the rest of the oil when necessary.

Food Facts

Like all dairy foods, milk is an excellent source of calcium and phosphorus, both of which are essential for healthy teeth and bones. Interestingly, there's exactly the same amount of calcium in skimmed milk as there is in whole milk. Zinc and B vitamins are also provided by milk along with antibodies which help boost the immune system and the digestive system.

milk

Preparation 15 mins • **Cooking** 12 mins • **Serves** 2-4

Baked Eggs and Ham

These pies are so simple to make and taste delicious. Traditional pastry is high in fat so this recipe uses ham as a base instead. Serve with ripe, juicy tomatoes or crunchy salad. They're perfect for brunch too.

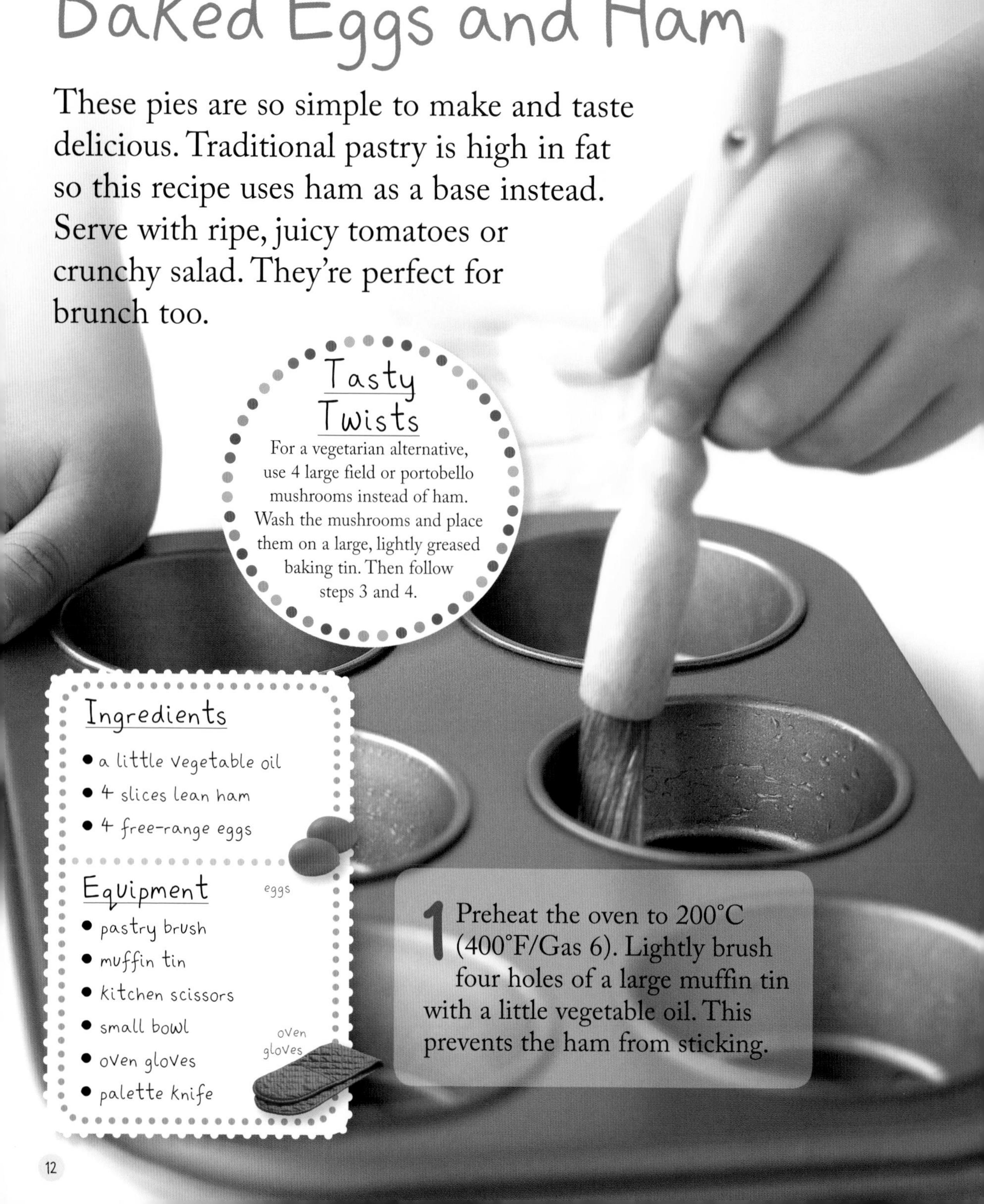

Tasty Twists

For a vegetarian alternative, use 4 large field or portobello mushrooms instead of ham. Wash the mushrooms and place them on a large, lightly greased baking tin. Then follow steps 3 and 4.

Ingredients

- a little vegetable oil
- 4 slices lean ham
- 4 free-range eggs

eggs

Equipment

- pastry brush
- muffin tin
- kitchen scissors
- small bowl
- oven gloves
- palette knife

oven gloves

1 Preheat the oven to 200°C (400°F/Gas 6). Lightly brush four holes of a large muffin tin with a little vegetable oil. This prevents the ham from sticking.

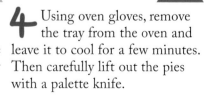

Did you know?
Pies have been around since ancient times. It is believed that the first ever pie recipe was published by the Romans and it was for rye-crusted goats cheese and honey pie.

boiled egg

Food Facts

Eggs can be cooked in many different ways. In this recipe the eggs are baked in the oven until set but they can also be fried, boiled, scrambled, or poached. To tell if an egg is fresh, place it in a bowl of water – if it sinks and lays flat it is fresh.

2 Arrange a slice of ham in each hole. Carefully trim the the slices to make them even, but make sure that the ham is still slightly above the edge of the tin.

3 One by one, crack an egg into a small bowl and pour it into each ham-lined hollow. Bake in the oven for 10–12 minutes, or until the egg has set.

4 Using oven gloves, remove the tray from the oven and leave it to cool for a few minutes. Then carefully lift out the pies with a palette knife.

Jewel Salad

Salad is delicious as a light meal or snack and can also be served as a nutritious accompaniment to a main meal.

Ingredients

cucumber

- 200g (7oz) couscous
- 300ml (½pt) hot vegetable stock
- 250g (9oz) cherry tomatoes
- ½ cucumber
- 1 medium sized pomegranate
- 30ml (2tbsp) olive oil
- grated zest and juice 1 lemon
- 1 small red onion (thinly sliced)
- 200g (7oz) feta cheese (crumbled)
  - large bunch (about 6tbsp) freshly chopped mint

olive oil

Equipment

- 3 bowls
- measuring jug
- fork
- chopping board
- knife

wooden spoon

- teaspoon
- wooden spoon

bowl

1 Place the couscous in a large bowl and pour over the hot stock and leave for 5 minutes until all the liquid has been absorbed. Allow to cool completely.

2 Cut the cherry tomatoes in half. Halve the cucumber lengthways and scoop out the seeds with a teaspoon, then cut into pieces.

3 Cut the pomegranate in half, and hold one half over a bowl. Lightly tap the pomegranate with a wooden spoon, until the seeds fall into the bowl.

4 Stir the lemon juice, zest and olive oil into the couscous. Add the tomatoes, cucumber, red onion, feta cheese and mint, then stir in the pomegranate seeds.

You can find pomegranates in the shops from October to January.

Chicken Pasta Salad

This mildly spiced pasta and chicken salad makes
a perfect light lunch or is ideal for a school
sandwich box.

Ingredients

- 125g (4oz) pasta bows
- 2 tsp sunflower oil
- 1 tbsp medium
  curry paste
- 3 spring onions (chopped)
- 1 ripe mango
  - juice of ¹/₂ lemon
  - 100ml (¹/₂ cup)
    low-fat yoghurt
  - 100ml (¹/₂ cup)
    mayonnaise
- 350g (12oz) cooked
  chicken breast (diced)
- 2 tbsp freshly
  chopped coriander
- 150g (5oz) mixed red
  and green grapes (halved)

lemon

pasta bows

Equipment

- large saucepan
- small frying pan
- wooden spoon
- knife
- mixing bowl

frying pan

1 Bring a large pan of lightly salted water to the boil. Add the pasta and cook according to package instructions. Drain and rinse under cold running water.

2 Meanwhile, in a small frying pan heat the oil, add the curry paste and spring onions, and cook for 2 minutes. Leave to cool.

4 Cut away the two sides of mango, close to the stone. Cut the flesh into criss-cross patterns, press each half inside out, and carefully cut off the cubes.

5 Place the spice mixture in a bowl and stir in the lemon juice, yoghurt, mayonnaise, and coriander. Add the chicken, mango, and grapes.

The spicy and sweet flavours in this pasta salad are a tasty combination.

Tasty
Twists
If you are a vegetarian,
just leave out the chicken.
Try adding tofu instead.

Tuna Quesadillas and Carrot Salad

Quesadillas are simple to prepare and taste great with a variety of interesting fillings. Best of all, they are delicious hot or cold.

Tasty Twists
For an equally colourful vegetarian alternative, try pesto, sliced tomato, and mozzarella.

Ingredients

- 2 soft flour tortillas
- 60g (2½ oz) canned tuna in spring water (drained)
- 40g (1½ oz) mature Cheddar (grated)
- 2 spring onions (peeled and sliced)

Cheddar cheese

- ½ small orange pepper (deseeded and cut into small pieces)
- a little olive oil

Carrot Salad
- 1 large carrot
- 2 tbsp raisins
- 1 tbsp pine nuts
- 1 tbsp olive oil
- 2 tsp lemon juice

spring onions

orange pepper

Equipment
- spoon
- chopping board
- frying pan
- spatula
- 2 dinner plates
- small sharp knife
- fork
- grater
- 2 mixing bowls

chopping board

frying pan

Food Facts

Tuna is an oily fish so it contains healthy omega-3 fats which are good for the brain, eyes, and skin. Tuna also provides vitamins B, D, and E.

tuna

1 Lay out one of the tortillas on a board or a clean and dry work surface. Leave a 2cm (¾in) border around the edge and spoon the tuna over the top.

2 Sprinkle the Cheddar cheese over the tuna and then add the spring onions and orange pepper. Place the second tortilla on top and press down firmly.

3 Brush a large frying pan with olive oil. Cook the quesadilla for 2 minutes over a medium heat. Press down with a spatula to make sure the cheese melts.

4 Now you need to turn the tortilla over. Carefully slide it onto a large plate. Put another plate on top and gently turn the plates over.

5 Carefully put the quesadilla back in the pan and cook the other side for 2 minutes. Remove the cooked quesadilla from the pan and cut it into wedges.

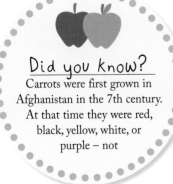

Did you know?
Carrots were first grown in Afghanistan in the 7th century. At that time they were red, black, yellow, white, or purple – not

1 Carefully grate the carrot and then put it into a bowl mixing bowl. Add the raisins and pine nuts to the bowl and mix everything together.

2 To make the dressing, mix together the olive oil and lemon juice using a fork. Pour the mixture over the carrot salad and stir to coat the salad evenly.

Colourful Seafood Salad

Protein, carbohydrates, vitamins, minerals, healthy fats – this salad has it all! In the green corner, avocadoes contain more protein than any other fruit and are also rich in beta-carotene and vitamin E. While in the red corner, tomatoes are good for your immune system and an excellent source of vitamins A, C, and E.

Tasty Twists

If you don't like prawns or can't get hold of them, cooked chicken is a healthy alternative. Vegetarians could add cooked tofu or pine nuts instead.

Ingredients

- 150g (5½ oz) pasta shells
- 250g (9oz) cooked peeled prawns
- 12 small tomatoes (quartered)
- 1 large avocado
- lettuce leaves (cut into strips)

tomatoes

Dressing:

- 4 tbsp mayonnaise
- 2 tsp lemon juice
- 2 tbsp tomato ketchup
- 2 drops Tabasco sauce (optional)
- salt and pepper

avocadoes

pasta shells

Equipment

- large saucepan
- wooden spoon
- small sharp knife
- chopping board
- mixing bowl
- small bowl
- teaspoon

mixing bowl

chopping board

1 Bring a large saucepan of water to the boil. Add the pasta and follow the cooking instructions on the packet. Drain well and leave to cool.

2 Carefully cut the avocado around its middle and gently prise it apart. Scoop out the stone with a teaspoon and then cut each half into quarters.

3 Peel off the skin and cut the avocado into chunks. Put the avocado into a bowl and spoon over half of the lemon juice to stop the fruit turning brown.

Although avocadoes are high in fat, it is the good monounsaturated kind.

4 Put the tomatoes, avocado, and prawns into a bowl with the pasta and season. Divide the shredded lettuce leaves between the serving bowls.

5 Mix together all the ingredients for the dressing in a small bowl. Add the pasta salad to the serving bowls and then drizzle over the dressing.

Food Facts

Like all shellfish, prawns are packed full of healthy minerals and are bursting with flavour. Prawns help to boost the immune system since they contain important minerals called zinc and selenium.

prawns

Veggie Spring Rolls

These crispy spring rolls filled with vegetables make an easy and delicious snack. Serve with sweet chilli dipping sauce or soy sauce if you prefer.

Ingredients

red pepper

- 100g (3¹/₂oz) beansprouts
- 50g (2oz) cabbage, shredded
- 1 carrot, cut into thin strips
- ¹/₂ red pepper, deseeded and thinly sliced
- 6 spring onions, thinly sliced

- 1 clove garlic, crushed
- 2.5cm (1in) piece root ginger, peeled and grated
- 15ml (1tbsp) dark soy sauce
- 6 sheets filo pastry
- 25g (1oz) melted butter

ginger

garlic

Equipment

knife

- mixing bowl
- wooden spoon
- chopping board
- knife
- small bowl
- pastry brush
- baking tray

cutting board

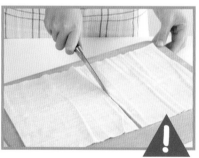

1 Preheat the oven to 190ºC, 375ºF, gas mark 5. In a large bowl, mix together all the ingredients, except the filo pastry and butter.

2 Place the sheets of pastry on top of each other and cut in half.

3 Place 1 sheet of the pastry on a board and brush the edges with a little of the melted butter. Place some of the filling on the bottom edge.

4 Roll up, folding the ends over. Repeat with remaining pastry and filling.

5 Place on a baking tray and brush with butter. Bake for 12 to 15 minutes until golden. Serve with sweet chilli dipping sauce.

Tasty Twists
You could try using sweetcorn, peas, or mushrooms if you prefer these fillings.

Serve these as a starter at a dinner party, or as a mid-afternoon snack!

Pitta Pockets

Tofu is a very versatile and nutritious ingredient. It naturally has a mild flavour but when marinated it takes on the flavour of the marinade. The sauce used in this recipe gives the tofu a delicious barbecue taste as well an appetising golden glow.

Did you know?
Tofu is also known as bean curd. Soya beans are cooked, puréed, and drained to produce a milky liquid. The liquid is mixed with a coagulant to form a custard or cheese-like substance.

Ingredients

tofu

pitta breads

- 250g (9oz) firm tofu
- a little olive oil
- 3 Cos lettuce leaves (shredded)
- 2 spring onions, peeled and cut into long strips
- a handful of alfalfa sprouts (optional)
- 4 wholemeal pitta bread (warmed in a toaster or warm oven)

For the marinade
- 2 tbsp sweet chilli sauce
- 2 tbsp tomato ketchup
- 2 tbsp soy sauce
- ½ tsp ground cumin

Equipment

- small sharp knife
- chopping board
- kitchen towel
- dessert spoon
- shallow dish
- griddle pan
- spatula or tongs

tongs

griddle pan

1 In a shallow dish, mix together all the ingredients for the marinade. Pat the tofu dry with a kitchen towel and then cut it into 8 long slices.

2 Put the tofu into the dish with the marinade. Spoon the marinade over the tofu until it is well coated. Leave the tofu to marinate for at least 1 hour.

3 Brush the griddle pan with a generous amount of olive oil and then put it on the heat. Carefully put 4 of the tofu slices into the hot pan.

Tasty Twists

Strips of chicken, pork, turkey, or beef or even a medley of vegetables such as pepper, courgette, and onion make a great alternative to the tofu.

Food Facts

Alfalfa is a seed with a long, slender shoot and a clover-like leaf that is usually bought as a sprouted plant. It is one of the few plants foods that is a complete protein and it is also an excellent source of vitamins B and C.

alfalfa

4 Cook the tofu for 4 minutes on each side, or until golden. As you cook, spoon over more of the marinade. Griddle the rest of the tofu in the same way.

5 Carefully slice along the edge of the pitta bread. Divide the lettuce, spring onions, and alfalfa sprouts between the pitta bread and then add 2 pieces of tofu.

Homemade Burgers

This tasty, low-fat turkey burger is a healthy winner when partnered with a high-fibre bun. It's sure to get gobbled up in no time!

Tasty Twists

Meat eaters could try pork, beef or lamb mince as a tasty alternative burger mix. Vegetarians could use a grilled portobello mushroom instead of a burger.

apple

wholemeal flour

wooden spoon

Ingredients

- 1 small onion
- 1 apple
- 450g (1lb) lean turkey, chicken, beef, pork, or lamb mince
- 1 small egg
- plain flour
- salt and pepper

To serve

- seeded burger buns (preferably wholemeal)
- lettuce leaves
- sliced tomatoes
- relish

Equipment

- grater
- mixing bowl
- wooden spoon
- small bowl
- fork or whisk
- cling film
- large plate
- tin foil
- tongs

burger buns

lettuce leaves

mixing bowl

1 Peel and then finely chop the onion. Leaving the skin on, grate the apple coarsely. When you can see the core and pips – it's done!

2 Put the onion and apple into a mixing bowl and add the mince. Stir or use your hands to break up the mince and mix it with the onion and apple.

3 Crack an egg into a separate bowl and lightly beat the yolk and white together, using a fork or whisk. This will help bind the burger mixture together.

4 Pour the beaten egg into the mince, onion, and apple mixture. Season, then using clean hands mix it all together – this part is messy but a lot of fun!

5 Lightly cover a plate and your hands with flour. Take a handful of the mixture and shape into a round, flat burger. Put it onto the floured plate.

6 Do the same with the rest of the mixture and then lightly dust all 6 burgers with flour. Cover with cling film and chill for at least 30 minutes.

Food Facts

Turkey is a versatile meat that contains an array of valuable nutrients. including iron, zinc and selenium. It is a good source of B vitamins, which are essential for the body's processing of foods. Turkey is also high in protein and low in fat, making it one of the healthiest meats of all.

turkey mince

7 Preheat the grill to medium. Place the burgers onto a foil-covered grill rack and cook them for 8 minutes on each side, or until cooked through.

Cheesy Potato Skins

Crispy bacon and melted cheese make these potato skins a firm favourite. If you and your friends don't like bacon, substitute it with tuna or chicken or leave it out completely.

Ingredients

cheddar cheese

- 4 large baking potatoes
- oil for brushing
- 8 rashers smoked streaky bacon
- 2.5ml ($\frac{1}{2}$tsp) paprika
- 50g (2oz) mature Cheddar cheese, grated
- 50g (2oz) mozzarella cheese, grated

- 6 spring onions, chopped

Dip:

- 150ml ($\frac{1}{4}$pt) sour cream
- 60ml (4tsp) fresh chives

onion

potatoes

Equipment

- fork
- pastry brush
- baking sheet
- knife
- chopping board
- wooden spoon
- frying pan
- 2 spoons
- small bowl

chopping board

Wooden spoon

1 Preheat the oven to 200°C, 400°F, gas mark 6. Prick the potatoes with a fork and brush them with oil. Bake for 1 hour, until cooked. Cool slightly.

2 Cut up the bacon rashers into small pieces. Place the bacon in a frying pan and dry fry, until lightly browned.

3 Cut the potatoes in half and scoop out the flesh with a spoon, leaving a thin layer. Cut each potato in half lengthways to make boat shapes.

4 Place on a baking sheet, season and sprinkle over a little paprika. Top with half of the bacon pieces. Mix together the cheeses and spring onions and sprinkle over the potatoes. Top with the remaining bacon.

5 Return the potato skins to the oven until golden. Cool for 10 minutes. Mix together the dip ingredients and serve with the skins.

Helpful Hints
Make sure the potatoes get really crispy in the oven – it will be worth the wait!

These easy-to-make filled potato skins are a delicious option for a party!

Butternut Squash Soup

This substantial soup is made from roasted butternut squash, but you could try it with pumpkin instead if you prefer.

This wholesome, warming soup is perfect for a cold day.

Ingredients

Vegetable oil

- 1 kg (2¼lb) butternut squash
- 15ml (1 tbsp) vegetable oil
- 1 onion (chopped)
- 600ml (20 fl oz) hot vegetable stock
- 30ml (2 tbsp) honey

To serve
- French stick
- Gruyére or Swiss cheese
- freshly chopped parsley

onion

Equipment

baking tray

- knife
- 3 spoons
- cutting board
- vegetable peeler
- baking tray
- food processor
- saucepan

knife

1 Preheat the oven to 200°C (400°F). Cut the butternut squash in half lengthwise, then, using a spoon, scoop out the seeds and pith.

2 Cut into large chunks, then, using a peeler, remove the skin. Cut the chunks into 2.5cm (1in) cubes.

3 Place on a baking tray, seasin with salt and freshly ground black pepper, then drizzle over the oil. Roast for 20 minutes, then remove from the oven.

4 Add the onion and stir. Return to the oven and cook for a further 15 minutes.

5 Place the butternut squash and onion in a food processor with half of the stock and blend until smooth.

6 Place the purée in a saucepan with the remaining stock and honey. Simmer for 3 to 4 minutes. Serve with slices of toasted French stick, cheese, and parsley.

Italian Pasta Soup

This wholesome, tasty soup is based on a traditional Italian soup called minestrone. With the pasta, vegetables, and Parmesan topping it is a complete meal in a bowl!

Minestrone was originally eaten by poor Italians and was made with whatever ingredients were available.

Tasty Twists

Meat eaters could add some bacon to the soup, but make sure you cook it thoroughly in step 3. Tinned mixed beans, green beans, courgettes or peppers would also taste great.

Ingredients

potatoes

- 75g (3oz) pasta bows
- 1 large onion
- 2 sticks celery
- 1 large carrot (scrubbed)
- 2 potatoes
- 1 tbsp olive oil
- 1 bay leaf
- 1 tsp dried oregano

- 1 litre (1¾ pints) vegetable stock
- 400g (14oz) canned chopped tomatoes
- Parmesan cheese (grated)

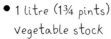

pasta bows

carrot

Equipment

- small sharp knife
- chopping board
- medium saucepan
- wooden spoon
- large saucepan with lid
- ladle

ladle

saucepan

Did you know?

Many people think that Venetian explorer Marco Polo introduced pasta to Italy from China in the 13th century. In fact, pasta has been eaten in Italy since as far back as Roman times!

1 Bring a medium-sized pan of water to the boil and add the pasta. Simmer until the pasta is just tender but not completely cooked. Drain well and set aside.

2 Chop the onion into small pieces. Peel the potatoes and cut them into bite-sized chunks. Slice the celery and carrot into bite-sized pieces.

Helpful Hints

When you drain the pasta in step 1, rinse it with cold water to prevent it sticking together and cooking further.

3 Heat the olive oil in a large saucepan. Add the onion and fry over a medium heat for 8 minutes or until it is softened and golden.

4 Next, add the celery, carrot, potatoes, oregano, and bay leaf then stir well. Pour in the stock and chopped tomatoes. Stir again and then bring to the boil.

Food Facts

Pasta is a carbohydrate food and it gives the body energy. Surprisingly it also provides a small amount of protein. It is best to use wholewheat pasta because it is higher in fibre, vitamins, and minerals than white pasta.

wholewheat pasta

5 When the soup is bubbling, reduce the heat to low. Half-cover the pan with a lid and simmer the soup for 15 minutes or until the potatoes are tender.

6 Remove the lid, add the pasta and stir well. Heat the pasta for 5 minutes. Ladle the soup into large bowls and sprinkle with Parmesan cheese.

Corn Chowder

This recipe will really warm you up on a cold day! Chowder is a special kind of thick soup from New England in the USA. Although some chowders include fish, this simple recipe relies on nutritious potatoes, sweetcorn, and carrot.

Helpful Hints

If you prefer a chunky soup, leave out step 5. For a smooth soup, blend all the mixture in step 5 until it is creamy.

potatoes

Ingredients

- 1 large onion
- 200g (9oz) fresh, frozen or tinned sweetcorn
- 1 large carrot
- 350g (12oz) potatoes
- 1 tbsp sunflower oil

onion

- 1 bouquet garni (optional)
- 1 bay leaf
- 1.2 litres (2 pints) vegetable stock
- 300ml (10fl oz) milk
- salt and pepper

carrot

Equipment

vegetable peeler

- small sharp knife
- vegetable peeler
- chopping board
- large saucepan with lid
- wooden spoon
- blender

wooden spoon

1 Peel and roughly chop the onion. Scrub the carrot and then thinly slice them. Finally, peel the potatoes and then cut them into small pieces.

2 Heat the oil in a saucepan. Add the onion and sauté over a medium heat for 8 minutes or until soft and slightly golden. Stir the onion occasionally.

3 Next, add the corn, carrot, potatoes, bouquet garni and bay leaf to the onions. Cook for 2 minutes, stirring constantly. Add the stock and bring to the boil.

Season your soup to taste with the salt and pepper.

Tasty Twists

Chunks of smoked haddock would add a delicious smoky flavour to this soup. Add the fish in step 4 with the milk and simmer for 5 minutes or until cooked.

Food Facts

Rich in complex carbohydrates, sweetcorn is also a good source of vitamins A, B, and C. If you use tinned sweetcorn in place of the fresh make sure you buy the type without added salt or sugar.

sweetcorn

4 Reduce the heat to medium to low. Cover with a lid and cook for 15 minutes, stirring occasionally. Add the milk and cook for a further 5 minutes.

5 Scoop out some of the vegetables and blend the rest of the soup until smooth. Return the vegetables and blended soup to the pan and warm through.

Club Sandwich

This club sandwich is made using ham, chicken, and cheese on toasted bread. However, you can use any combination of your favourite meats or cheeses.

This is a super deluxe sandwich perfect for a luxurious lunch! —

Ingredients

iceberg
lettuce

- 4 slices white bread
- 2 slices wholemeal bread
- 4 tbsp mayonnaise
- 1 tbsp lemon juice
- 100ml (3½ fl oz) milk
- 50g (2oz) shredded iceberg lettuce

- 2 slices ham
- 2 slices Swiss or Cheddar cheese
- 1 tomato (sliced)
- 50g (2oz) cooked chicken breast (shredded)

lemon

wholemeal
bread

Equipment

mixing
bowl

- bread knife
- cutting board
- mixing bowl
- metal spoon
- toothpicks

cutting board

1 Lightly toast the bread on both sides under a preheated moderate grill or in a toaster. Cut off the crusts.

2 In a small bowl mix together the mayonnaise and lemon juice. Season to taste. Stir in the shredded lettuce.

3 Spread 2 slices of the white toast with half of the lettuce and mayonnaise mixture.

4 Place a slice of ham, then a slice of cheese on top of each. Top with the wholemeal bread, spread with the remaining lettuce and mayonnaise.

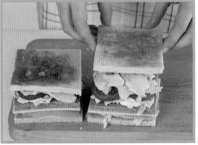

5 Add some slices of tomato and the chicken. Top with the remaining white toast.

6 Cut each sandwich into 4 triangles and secure each with a toothpick.

Pesto Pasta

Pasta is the ultimate quick, simple, and nutritious meal. Try stirring in a spoonful of homemade pesto for an equally quick and mouthwateringly tasty sauce.

Tasty Twists

Peas, green beans, carrots, or cauliflower could be used instead of the broccoli. Meat eaters could add some cooked chicken or bacon.

You could swirl a spoonful of pesto in soup, stir it into bread dough, or spread it over toast.

Ingredients

- 250g (9oz) spaghetti
- 15-20 small florets broccoli

Pesto:
- 2 large cloves garlic (roughly chopped)
- 3 tbsp pine nuts
- 4 tbsp fresh finely grated Parmesan cheese (plus extra for serving)
- 60g (2½ oz) fresh basil leaves
- 75ml (3fl oz) olive oil
- salt and pepper

spaghetti   salt   pepper

pine nuts

garlic

 basil leaves

Equipment

- small sharp knife
- chopping board
- food processor
- jar with a lid
- large saucepan
- wooden spoon
- colander
- pasta spoon

 colander

 chopping board

1 Put the garlic and pine nuts in a food processor and blend until coarsely chopped. Next, add the Parmesan and basil and blend again until a coarse purée.

2 Pour the olive oil into the food processor and blend to make a smooth mixture. Season to taste. Transfer the pesto to a jar with a lid.

Did you know?

Pesto is an Italian sauce from the city of Genoa. It dates back to Roman times. The word "pesto" comes from an Italian word meaning "to crush".

3 Fill a large saucepan three-quarters full of water. Add 1 teaspoon of salt and bring the water to the boil. Lower the pasta into the pan.

4 Cook the pasta according to the instructions on the packet. About 4 minutes before the pasta is cooked, add the broccoli and simmer.

5 Drain the pasta and broccoli but reserve 2 tablespoons of the cooking water. Return the pasta and broccoli to the pan with the cooking water.

Food Facts

Broccoli is a super-veg thanks to its impressive range of nutrients, from B vitamins and iron to zinc and potassium. Broccoli belongs to the same family as cabbage, cauliflower, kale, and brussel sprouts.

broccoli

6 Add enough pesto to coat the pasta and broccoli (you may have a some leftover). Stir and divide the pasta between four shallow bowls.

Rainbow Beef

Stir-frying is a quick and easy way to make a colourful and nutritious meal. You could also serve this stir-fry with rice instead of noodles.

Did you know?
Mangetout means "eat everything" in French, and they are so called because you eat the whole vegetable, including the pod. Mangetout are also called snow peas.

Ingredients

- 300g (10½oz) lean beef (cut into thin strips)
- 1 tbsp sunflower oil
- 250g (9oz) medium egg noodles
- 1 red pepper (deseeded and cut into thin strips)
- 6 baby corn (halved)
- 75g (3oz) mangetout
- 3 spring onions (sliced on the diagonal)
- 2 cloves garlic (chopped)
- 2 tsp grated fresh ginger
- 4 tbsp fresh orange juice

Marinade:
- 6 tbsp hoisin sauce
- 2 tbsp soy sauce
- 1 tbsp runny clear honey
- 1 tsp sesame oil

baby corn

mangetout

noodles

Equipment

- small sharp knife
- chopping board
- spoon
- shallow dish
- wok or large frying pan
- spatula or wooden spoon
- tongs
- medium saucepan
- colander

tongs

colander

Food Facts

Stir-frying is a healthy method of preparing food because the ingredients are cooked quickly in a minimum amount of oil. This keeps the fat levels down and retains vital vitamins and minerals which are often destroyed by long cooking times.

wok

1 Put the marinade ingredients in a shallow dish. Mix them together and then add the beef strips. Coat them in the marinade, cover and set aside for 1 hour.

2 Heat the sunflower oil in a wok or frying pan. Remove the beef from the marinade using tongs and carefully put it into the wok or frying pan.

Tasty Twists

Strips of pork and chicken are a good alternative to the beef, or you could try prawns or tofu. For the best flavour, it's important to marinate them first.

3 Stirring continuously, fry the beef on a high heat for 1½ minutes or until browned all over. Remove the beef using the tongs and set aside.

4 Bring a saucepan of water to the boil. Add the noodles to the water, stir to separate them and then cook according to the packet instructions until tender.

5 Add a little more oil to the wok if it looks dry. Add the red pepper, baby corn, mangetout, and spring onions. Stir-fry for 2 minutes.

6 Add the garlic, ginger, beef, and the leftover marinade and stir-fry for 1 minute. Pour in the orange juice, and cook, stirring, for another minute.

7 Drain the noodles in a colander and divide them between 4 shallow bowls. Spoon the vegetable and beef stir-fry over the noodles and serve.

Salmon Parcels

Salmon is full of brain-boosting, healthy oils that help with concentration and memory. If you are not usually a fan of fish, this tasty recipe is sure to win you over!

Did you know?
Japan consumes the highest amount of salmon per person, and has the lowest level of heart disease in the world.

Vegetarians could use a selection of vegetables such as carrot, red pepper, mangetout, broccoli, spring onions, or courgettes.

Ingredients

carrot

- 2 tbsp sesame seeds
- 4 slices fresh ginger (peeled and cut into thin strips)
- 2 tbsp soy sauce
- 4 tbsp orange juice
- 4 thick salmon fillets (about 150g/5¹/₂oz each)
- 1 carrot (cut into thin strips)
- 1 red pepper (deseeded and cut into thin strips)
- 3 spring onions (cut into thin strips)
- salt and black pepper
- 250g (9oz) noodles

fresh ginger

noodles

Equipment

sharp knife

- small sharp knife
- chopping board
- frying pan
- baking tray
- baking paper

chopping board

1 Preheat the oven to 200°C (400°F/Gas 6). Toast the sesame seeds in a dry frying pan until golden. Remove from the pan and set aside.

2 Cut the baking parchment into 4 pieces, at least twice the size of the salmon fillets. Place each piece of salmon on a piece of baking parchment.

3 Arrange a mixture of the carrot, red pepper, spring onion, and ginger strips on top of each salmon fillet. Drizzle over the soy sauce and orange juice.

4 Season with salt and pepper. Carefully fold in the top and bottom of each parcel and then gather up the sides. Gently fold to make 4 loose parcels.

5 Put the parcels on a baking tray and bake for 15 minutes. Add the noodles to a pan of boiling water and cook, following the instructions on the packet.

Tasty Twists

Chicken breasts would also taste delicious cooked in this way. Follow the recipe but bake the chicken slightly longer than the salmon – about 20–25 minutes, or until cooked through.

6 Remove the fish from the oven and leave to cool slightly before opening the parcels. Serve with the noodles and a sprinkling of sesame seeds.

Food Facts

Salmon is an excellent source of polyunsaturated fatty acids, known as omega-3. These are the healthier kind of fats and have been shown to help reduce heart disease and are good for the brain, skin, eyes, and nerves too.

salmon

Fruit Sundae

This fruity ice cream sundae is a refreshing, vitamin-filled treat. Any of your favourite fruits will taste great in this recipe and if you don't have yoghurt ice cream, you can use a fruit-flavour ice cream instead.

Helpful Hints
Try to buy strawberries in season for the best, most nutritious fruit. The lemon juice enhances the flavour of the strawberries and also prevents the sauce oxidising or discolouring.

Ingredients

- 8 small scoops yoghurt ice cream
- 4 small scoops vanilla ice cream
- a selection of fresh fruit, such as strawberries, mango, kiwi fruit or raspberries (the amount depends on size of your glasses)
- toasted flaked almonds (optional)

Strawberry Sauce:
- 350g (12oz) strawberries (hulled)
- squeeze of fresh lemon juice
- a little icing sugar

mango

raspberries

Equipment

- sharp knife
- chopping board
- sieve
- blender or food processor
- ice cream scoop
- 4 sundae glasses

kiwi

banana

1 First make the Strawberry Sauce. Slice the strawberries in half and then purée them in a blender until they form a smooth sauce with no lumps.

2 Press the strawberry purée through a sieve, using the back of a spoon, to remove the seeds. Stir in a little lemon juice and some icing sugar to sweeten.

3 Put a scoop of yoghurt ice cream into the glass and add a spoonful of Strawberry Sauce. Add some fruit and a scoop of vanilla ice cream.

4 Add more sauce and fruit and then top the sundae with a scoop of yoghurt ice cream and a sprinkling of nuts. Repeat to make three more sundaes.

Food Facts

Strawberries are a good source of vitamin C, which is excellent for your skin, hair, and nails and also helps to boost your immune system.

strawberries

- **Preparation** 10 mins   • **Cooking** 6 mins   • **Serves** 4

Griddled Fruit & Honey

You will love this fruit griddled – it helps bring out the sweetness. If you don't have a griddle pan, place the fruit under a hot grill.

Ingredients

- 3 peaches
- 4 apricots
- 30ml (2tbsp) caster sugar
- 2.5ml (1/2tsp) ground cinnamon
- 200ml (7floz) Greek yogurt
- 30ml (2tbsp) clear honey

caster sugar

peaches

ground cinnamon

Equipment

- knife
- chopping board
- 2 mixing bowls
- 2 metal spoons
- griddle pan
- tongs

mixing bowl

tongs

1 Cut each peach in half and remove the stone. Then cut each into quarters. Halve the apricots and remove the stones.

2 In a large bowl, mix together the sugar and cinnamon, then add the fruit. Toss to coat in the sugar mixture.

3 Preheat a griddle pan and add the peaches, flesh side down. Cook for 2 to 3 minutes. Add the apricots, and turn over the peaches. Cook until caramelised.

4 Meanwhile, place the yogurt in a bowl and pour over the honey. Stir to create a rippled effect. Serve the warmed griddled fruit with the yogurt and honey dip.

Tasty
Twists
If you don't like
Greek yogurt, try this
with ice cream or
crème fraiche.

Slices of mango and pineapple are also delicious griddled.

Acknowledgements

The publisher would like to thank the following:
Photography assistants Jon Cardwell, Michael Hart and Ria Osborne.

Young chefs and fantastic hand models: Efia Brady, Ella Bukbardis, Eleanor Bullock, Megan Craddock, Elise Flatman, Eliza Greenslade, George Greenslade, Mykelia Hill, Eva Mee, Grace Mee, Hannah Moore, Shannon O'Kelly, Gabriella Soper, Rachel Tilley, Charlotte Vogel and Hope Wadman.

All images © Dorling Kindersley
For further information see: **www.dkimages.com**